STEAMPUNK DEVICES
COLORING BOOK

JEREMY ELDER

DOVER PUBLICATIONS, INC.
MINEOLA, NEW YORK

NOTE

Originally coined to describe fantasy and science fiction in steam-powered settings, the term "steampunk" has come to identify an aesthetic movement. Its campy rendition of Victorian style blends elements of technology and romance, and its influence extends from literature and art to music and fashion. Now you can create your own steampunk masterpieces by coloring the 31 illustrations in this book. Beautifully rendered by artist Jeremy Elder, these images will entice not only devotees of steampunk, but any colorist who likes bold and imaginative drawings.

Bibliographical Note
Steampunk Devices Coloring Book is a new work, first published by Dover Publications, Inc., in 2014.

International Standard Book Number
ISBN-13: 978-0-486-49443-2
ISBN-10: 0-486-49443-8

Manufactured in the United States by Courier Corporation
49443801   2014
www.doverpublications.com

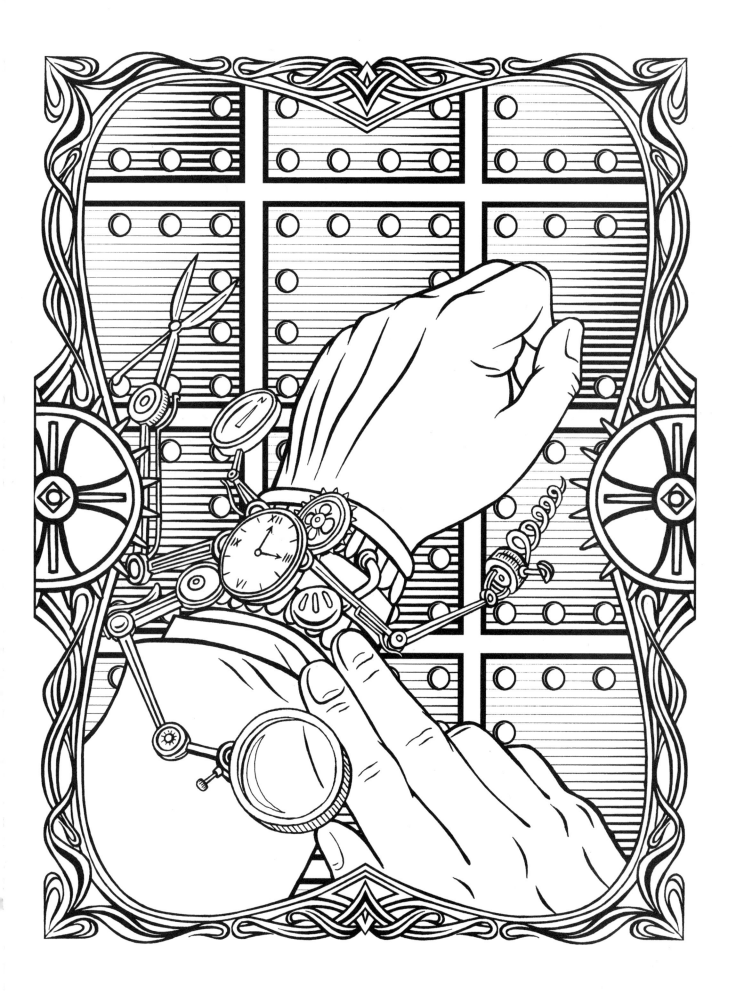

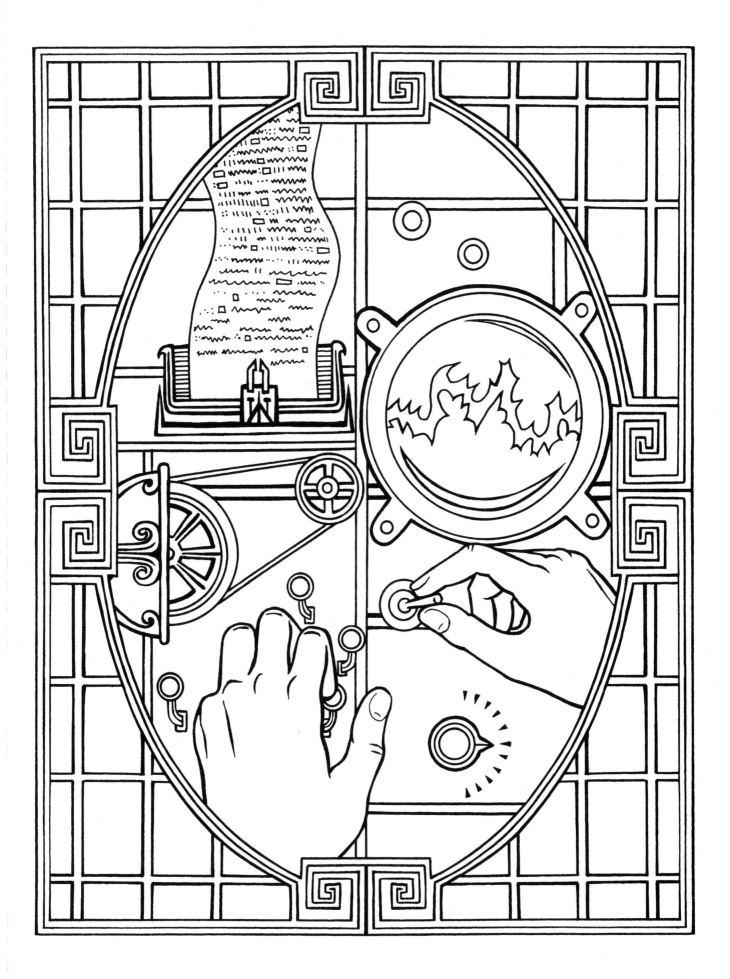